God's Power Revealed Through Prayer

TRUE LIFE STORIES

Nancy Berthiaume LaPierre

TEACH Services, Inc.
P U B L I S H I N G
www.TEACHServices.com • (800) 367-1844

World rights reserved. This book or any portion thereof may not be copied or reproduced in any form or manner whatever, except as provided by law, without the written permission of the publisher, except by a reviewer who may quote brief passages in a review.

The author assumes full responsibility for the accuracy of all facts and quotations as cited in this book. The opinions expressed in this book are the author's personal views and interpretations, and do not necessarily reflect those of the publisher.

This book is provided with the understanding that the publisher is not engaged in giving spiritual, legal, medical, or other professional advice. If authoritative advice is needed, the reader should seek the counsel of a competent professional.

Copyright © 2018 Nancy Berthiaume LaPierre
Copyright © 2018 TEACH Services, Inc.
ISBN-13: 978-1-4796-0948-2 (Paperback)
ISBN-13: 978-1-4796-0949-9 (ePub)
Library of Congress Control Number: 2018941581

Unless otherwise indicated, all Scripture quotations are from the New King James Version® (NKJV), copyright © 1982 by Thomas Nelson. Used by permission. All rights reserved

Nancy Berthiaume LaPierre (1954–) author of *Journey to a Better Land* and *Courage for the Soul of the Caregiver* (available at www.nblbooks.com). *Journey to a Better Land* audiobook available at audible.com. *Journey to a Better Land* paper back and Kindle versions, available at Amazon.com.

Published by

www.TEACHServices.com • (800) 367-1844

This Book is Dedicated…

To my husband and three children, who always inspire me to be the best wife and mother. To my brother Dennis because, if it were not for almost losing him to death, I would not have written this book. Thank you, Dennis, for showing me how really powerful our God is and how prayer works.

Thank you all for teaching me the true meaning of the motto:

"Much Prayer, Much Power. Little Prayer, Little Power. No Prayer, No Power."

Love you forever and always!

Contents

Preface . . . .*vii*

Acknowledgements . . . . *viii*

Article 1: Jesus in My Heart—From Chaos to Peace 9

Article 2: Torn Between Two Loves and Making the Right Choice . . .12

Article 3: The Search for Truth: Standing Up for God 15

Article 4: An Overwhelming Test. 18

Article 5: The Green Pepper 22

Article 6: The Big Blue Bus and the Sign 25

Article 7: The Prayed-for Home .30

Article 8: A Promise of Hope. 33

Article 9: Our Beloved Cat Sam's Eulogy 37

Article 10: The Forks in the Road 40

Article 11: The Letter. 43

Article 12: Tragedy Strikes the Family 47

Article 13: Another Powerful Lesson to be Learned 51

Article 14: "Peaches," the Angel Kitty. 55

Article 15: The Finest Hours: Preparing the Heart 59

Article 16: Dealing with Uncertainty. 64

Preface

Dear Reader,

As you read these stories that I have compiled for you, it is my hope that you know and experience the true meaning of the power of prayer and that you become aware that we serve a living and real God who cares. He has your best interest at heart. He wants to be your friend, your caregiver, your parent, your protector, and more. He wants you to rely on Him for all your needs, and, yes, even your wants. As His child, bring your petitions to Him no matter how small or big, and He will open the way for you. Through the power of prayer, you will see how great our God is. Won't you give it a try today? He will not fail you.

God bless you.
Nancy

Acknowledgements

I would like to acknowledge God's influence in helping me write this book. He was the one who gently prodded me to sit down and write, though I constantly resisted. My brother Dennis may have unknowingly been the inspiration for starting the manuscript, but it was God who kept after me to continue to the end. I want to thank Him for always being there for me—no matter the situation—and for showing me how really powerful prayer is. I also want to thank Hannelore for planting the seed in my mind to write out the stories that would be compiled for this book. She was always praying with me for my brother. Then, as we witnessed God's power in making him better, she suggested that I write our Jim's story and share it with others because they really need to know that God answers prayer.

A special "thank you" to Jean and her daughter, Elizabeth, for allowing me to use Elizabeth's baptismal picture to represent Jesus in my heart. Thank You, God, for bringing that family into my life again just when I would need them most— yet another witness to the power of prayer.

Jesus in My Heart—
From Chaos to Peace

*Take My yoke upon you and learn from Me,
for I am gentle and lowly in heart, and you will find rest
for your souls. For My yoke is easy and My burden is light.*
—**Matthew 11:29, 30**

1

A young girl is filled with fear and anger as she is raised in an abusive, alcoholic, dysfunctional home. Her continual prayer is to find a better life than the one she is now experiencing. She is determined not to follow in her parents' footsteps, but she does not know how to find a better way. That young girl was me.

Dad drank and smoked and went to bars all the time. Mom was pretty miserable with it all but followed in his footsteps. They raised five children in this very dysfunctional home. However, they did not start this way. Mom was only fifteen when she met dad. He was eighteen years old and a Christian who always carried his Bible everywhere he went. But then he joined the military and served for two years. When he was discharged, he was a changed man and not for the better. He had begun smoking and drinking. By then, Mom was seventeen. The two were still very much in love, so they decided to get married. It took a few years before Dad found God again. Everything was happy for a while because they really loved each other and had God in the middle of their relationship.

Then, one day, Dad found a job welding at a foundry. He met a lot of non-Christian people there, and they became his new friends. They would invite him to go with them to bars. If he didn't want to go, they would say he was henpecked. Dad did not want to be thought of as being henpecked, so he would give in and do what his friends asked him to do. Sadly, my parent's marriage, which had such a great start, ended in tragedy.

At times, my home was not a very pleasant place. When Dad got drunk, he was not very nice. He could get very mean, and sometimes he would try to hurt us. When Mom could not deal with it all, she would go into her own little world and try to forget what was going on around her. My older sister and I had to become the caregivers of our younger siblings, which made it very hard on us.

One day, a door-to-door salesman came to our house selling Christian books. One set of books he was selling was the ten-book Bible Story set.

It took a little persuasion, but I finally convinced Mom to buy those books for me.

I was so happy and thankful to get those books! I read the whole set to my younger siblings, explaining everything I could, trying to show them the love of God, and telling them that there was more to life than what we were seeing at home. I told them there was a loving God watching over us and that He cared that we were hurting. At last, we had a place to go to get away from the hurtful surroundings of our lives. When we would sit together with those books, we were brought into a peaceful place, and I would thank God for touching Mom's heart to allow her to say, "Yes, we can buy those books."

> *I told them there was a loving God watching over us and that He cared that we were hurting.*

My grandmother, Dad's mom, was another happy place in our lives. She was a wonderful, caring Christian woman and a big role model to all of us. She would take us to church and would always read the Bible to us.

I started to see the hand of God working in my life in a more noticeable way. I relied on my grandmother for all the guidance I could get. Whenever I had a problem, I would go see her, and she would pray with me, open God's Word, and God would always answer her prayers. She had a special gift. I trusted her completely. Through her influence, I started to really know God and how much He cared for His children.

I was baptized at the age of thirteen, fully accepting Christ as my Savior. That was such a happy day! Even at that young age, I realized that God was answering my prayers, helping me find that better way. I just had to trust Him and let Him lead. This was only the beginning of what God had in store for me. I learned that it is not only the destination that is important in our life but also the journey that takes us there.

Torn Between Two Loves and Making the Right Choice

Hear my prayer, O LORD, give ear to my supplications!
In Your faithfulness answer me, and in your righteousness.
— **Psalm 143:1**

2

Choices! Sometimes the choices we make are good; sometimes they are not so good. Making good decisions throughout our life is a great challenge. If we make the wrong choice, unmindful of what the consequences may be, it can affect not only us but also those around us and even future generations. One of the biggest choices I had to make was about who I would spend the rest of my life with. If I made the wrong choice, it surely could have had disastrous results for me.

As a young girl, I learned the power of prayer. When it came to making important choices, like finding the right mate, I knew I had to spend many hours in prayer seeking to know God's will. Would I listen to God and what He was telling me through prayer, or would I ignore what He was telling me and try to make my own decisions?

When I was seventeen, I met a young college student who was going to be a Baptist minister. He was four years older than I was. We dated for three years, and I really thought he was the one for me. Then, for some unknown reason, we broke up, and I was devastated. As I was recovering from this devastation, I was invited to some Bible studies, which is something I really needed to start my healing process. Those attending were a great bunch of young people my own age, and we had such a wonderful time together. However, my beliefs were slightly different from theirs, and that difference caused some disagreements.

One day I decided that I was tired of the disagreements and that the best course would be to leave the group. On the night that I was going to make my announcement to say goodbye, there was a knock on the door of the meeting. We opened it to find two young men standing there. They explained that they heard that we were having a Bible study and asked if it would be okay if they joined us. We told them "Sure!" At the end of the study, one of the young men, whose name was Mark, turned to me and playfully said, "Hi, do you want to get married?" and I said, "Yes." We set a date that very moment. From then on we dated, and I thought I was falling in love again.

Yes, I *knew* I was falling in love again. However, I still had some fond thoughts that would not go away concerning my first love. One day, as I was

> *At the end of the study, one of the young men, whose name was Mark, turned to me and playfully said, "Hi, do you want to get married?"*

working around my home, the telephone rang and I answered it. I could not believe the voice on the other end. It was my first love, asking me if I wanted to go somewhere with him. He had some deliveries to make, and he desperately wanted to talk with me. Part of my heart wanted to say, "Yes," but another part of me was saying, "No, this is not a good thing to do." My mom, who really loved Mark, was standing right beside me, shaking her head. She thought Mark was doing me a world of good, helping me get all the healing I needed from my past. She did not want to see me slipping back again. I listened that day to my mom and did not go out with my old boyfriend.

Mark and I continued dating and decided, in earnest, to get married. I still had some doubts creeping in, and every night I would get on my knees and plead with God to help me make the right choice. Then, one night, God answered me in a big way. I went to bed and, sometime during the night, God gave me a dream. In my dream, I was on a lake with those men that I thought I loved. As we were rowing across the lake, both men fell out of the boat. The water was fairly deep and neither one of them could swim, at least, not in my dream. All of a sudden they started yelling for help because they were drowning. I was the only one who could save them. I saw myself jumping out of the boat to try to save them. Since the men were far apart from each other, I could not save them both. My heart went out to my old love, but, with all the strength I could muster, I started in Mark's direction. I was determined to save him, even if it meant letting the other one go. It was a sad realization, but, when I woke up from that powerful dream, I knew, beyond a shadow of a doubt, who it was that I was supposed to spend the rest of my life with.

Oh, the power of prayer! By listening to God, I found myself learning the true meaning of love. I was about to embark on new and exciting adventures that would eventually lead me to a much more fulfilled life, one with peace and happiness in it. Thank you, Jesus!

The Search for Truth: Standing Up for God

You search the Scriptures, for in them you think you have eternal life; and these are they which testify of Me.
—John 5:39

3

Dreams can be a very powerful tool. As I pointed out in the last story, I learned that God sometimes uses dreams to speak to us, just as he did in the days of Daniel. God had given me a dream that helped me to choose who I was going to spend the rest of my life with, and I have never been sorry for the choice I made so many years ago. God knew what the best choice was, and the outcome was wonderful.

Now, let's go back to the Bible study where I met my husband-to-be. Let's go back before that night—before the knock on the door that changed my life completely. As I stated earlier, I did not agree with some of the things these young people were saying. Whenever I tried to give them my point of view, they dismissed it. They never wanted to hear what I had to say. The leaders felt they were right, and they made it clear that we were all there just to love Jesus and study His Word. The interpretations of each subject were strictly their own, and they did not appreciate it if anyone expressed a different view.

Quietly I prayed for these sincere young people. I continued going week after week, trying to participate the best I could. After the study, I would go home feeling like I had just betrayed my Lord. This went on for many months. Then one night, after I got back home, I went to bed and had another very powerful dream. God knew that I was struggling with some of the things that were being said at the Bible study. In my dream, I saw the finger of God pointing to a huge plaque with the Ten Commandments on it. On one side of the plaque, I could see a dark figure like a shadow looming over me. I remember looking at the evil figure and then at God's finger pointing to the commandments. When I woke up, I knew what God wanted me to do. He wanted me to stand for His truth, to choose light and not darkness (John 14:15, 21).

How would I ever go back to say goodbye to this group of people that did not have a clue how they made me feel? They were not hearing me, and I truly believed that God wanted me to leave. The following week, with a prayer in my heart that God would show me how to talk to them without creating hard feelings, I left for the study. This was not going to be an easy thing. Despite everything, there was a certain bond among the members of the group. When I first met these young people, I was going through some devastating things, and they were the ones who helped me get through it. But what was I going to do?

God saved me from having to do anything that night because that very night I met my husband-to-be, Mark. Afterward, I continued to go back to the meeting because I wanted to see him more. As I saw how interested in Bible truth he was, I asked him if he would like to study from a set of lessons that I had. The lessons had more in-depth study than what we were getting with the group. He agreed, and we studied the lessons together, searching the Bible for the truth. If we disagreed with something in the lessons, we would pray together and search the Scriptures to find out what God wanted to teach us. It was so different from having to listen to others tell us what they thought about certain subjects without giving us a chance to study for ourselves.

Then came the day that we both said goodbye to our caring friends. It was no longer difficult for me to do this because I had Mark by my side. I did not have to do it alone. I am so thankful that God heard and answered my prayers and my concerns by sending me dreams. He not only helped me to find a good way to say "Goodbye," but He also helped me choose a lifelong mate who would stand by me for the rest of my life. Thank you, God, for answered prayers through dreams.

An Overwhelming Test

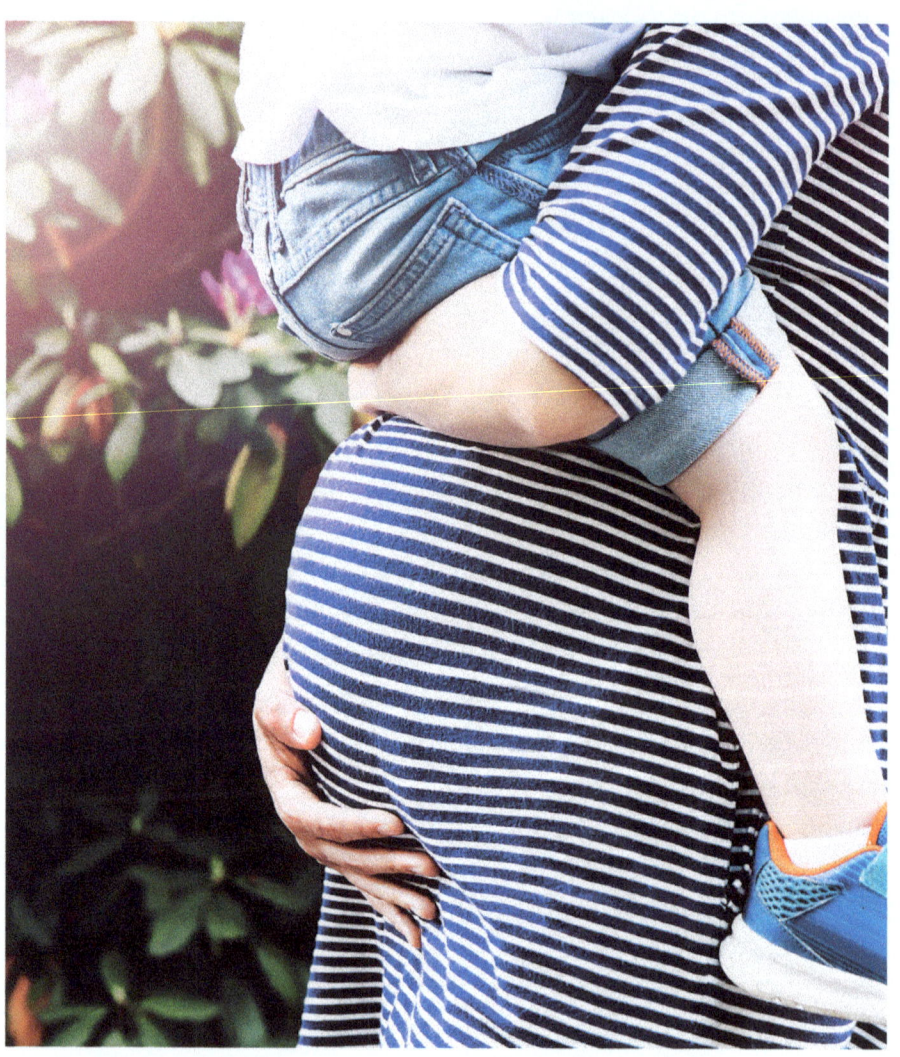

Therefore I say to you, whatever things you ask when you pray, believe that you receive them, and you will have them.
—Matthew 11:24

4

At this early stage of our marriage, we were about to encounter changes. Some of these changes were good; some were not. A year had gone by since we were married, and I had found myself "in the family way." We were so happy to be having our first child. Then one night—after three months of pregnancy—something happened. I was having pain and bleeding. Mark rushed me to the hospital only to hear the dreaded word—*miscarriage!* We were devastated! We cried, and I asked myself, *Would we ever be able to start a family? Would I be able to carry any more children?* The doctors were not too sure, and Mark and I were grieving over the loss of our little one. What had happened? Would it happen again? Only God knew, and only time would tell.

After that awful period in our lives, we decided that it was time to go house hunting. We had been staying with my mom and dad to save money for the perfect house. We had no children and were free to go anywhere we wanted. We prayed about it and ended up choosing to live in Connecticut. We found a nice little neighborhood under construction with the cutest little houses popping up everywhere. We settled on a house that was not yet finished. Everything about our buying the house was falling into place. What a thrill to watch it all unfold and know that the house would be ours someday! Then came the day that the house was finally finished enough for us to move in. We were so happy! We finally could settle down and possibly start a family.

After a few months of living there, something wonderful did happen. I found myself "in the family way" again. But it was not an easy pregnancy. I had morning sickness that lasted all day every day right until the time of the delivery. My sickness was hard on Mark as well. He had to go to work every day, leaving me alone to cope with everything, which was not good at all. I eventually had to go live with my mom in Rhode Island for the extra care I needed. Mark and I were away from each other for many months, only visiting on weekends. Then came the day that I felt well enough to go back home. Our baby was three and a half weeks overdue, and we thought

I would be pregnant forever. Finally, our baby boy did arrive, and life was really good. We could not have been happier!

Then, eleven months later, I found myself "in the family way" again. Oh, no! This was much too early. I felt just as sick as in the last pregnancy, but I was determined to stay at home to be able to care for my baby and husband.

During those months of carrying our second child, I decided to get my babysitting license because the financial load was just too much for Mark to handle alone. I thought I could help him by getting a job that would allow me to stay at home with my son. I found out quick enough that I could not do it. I was still sick, and my first-born was a handful, to say the least. At times I would have four or five babies in the house, all needing my attention. I became totally overwhelmed. One day, when I was praying for help and guidance, I took the Bible, opened its pages, and was led to Isaiah 41:10, which reads, "Fear not, for I am with you; be not dismayed, for I am your God. I will strengthen you, Yes, I will help you, I will uphold you with My righteous right hand." I thanked God for His immediate answer. I don't know how many times I have claimed that promise through the years. Our Father is an awesome God, and He does care about us, no matter the situation.

Again, my due date came and went. Three and a half weeks overdue, son number two was finally born. It was not easy to take care of two little ones. My youngest had a problem, and we were at a loss to know what to do. He would cry a lot and frequently threw temper tantrums. I took him to the doctor for help, but he was at a loss as well. We just had to wait it out, praying that someday our baby would grow out of it. Mark and I felt so awful not being able to help our little one. We knew something was wrong but could not bring him relief or even comfort him. The more we did, the worse he got.

Sometime during this period, my grandmother came for a visit. We were all excited! She was going to be with us for a while. During her visits, she saw what was going on with our little one, and she told me, "We need to pray for him." I told her we always do that, but she said, "We are going to pray anyway, and God is going to answer our prayers." It seemed that her faith was so much stronger than either Mark's or mine. We knelt down together and prayed for our baby son. When we were finished, I called my little son in for lunch and knew that the temper tantrums would normally be starting soon. Uncharacteristically everything I asked him to do he did without a single complaint. The temper fits, for the most part, had ended. I could not believe it! I was so thankful to God and to my grandmother for allowing our lives to be much quieter from then on. Thank God for the power of prayer.

> *We knelt down together and prayed for our baby son.*

The Green Pepper

*A man's heart plans his way,
but the Lord directs his steps.*
—**Proverbs 16:9**

5

As we raised our two boys, we were determined to teach them how to rely on God for anything they were going through, whether the problem they were facing was big or small. Little things are important too! We tried to show them that we serve a living God who cares for us. Even as we go about our busy day not even thinking about Him, He is always thinking about us. Following is an amazing story about how God watches over His children.

One hot August day, Mark and I, with our two little ones who were five and three, decided to go for a walk to the store to buy some much-needed things. Our family car was broken at the time or we surely would not have chosen to walk in the heat. We were not thinking about how long it would take us to walk with two little ones. We took no food or water; we just had ourselves, and off we went.

We were having a wonderful time, talking and looking at God's creation, when suddenly one of my little ones started complaining about how thirsty he was. His complaining was turning into a voice of panic. Then the other one joined in. I knew that, hot as it was, we still had a long way to go. There were no houses anywhere in sight; there were only trees on either side of the road we were on. I started to panic and prayed to God. How could we have been so foolish to have left the house without proper provisions for our little ones when it was so hot? I was beginning to think about how this could end in tragedy for my boys. Mark and I stopped and prayed to the only source of help that we knew of, asking for His forgiveness, and for His help, if He could please find a way to do so. We ended our prayer and resumed our walking,

I started to panic and prayed to God. How could we have been so foolish to have left the house without proper provisions for our little ones when it was so hot?

feeling content that God was in control and that He would take care of the situation.

The kids did not stop their complaining, but we knew how to trust the only One who could give us the help we needed. We had not walked very far when, all of a sudden, in our path was a big, beautiful green pepper. Where did it come from? As I stated earlier, there were no houses anywhere near the pathway we were taking. This was amazing! What an answer to our prayer for what we were going through at that moment. With thankful hearts, we picked up the pepper and with our hands divided it up the best we could. Oh, how wonderfully refreshing that pepper was! It quenched all of our thirsts just fine as we continued our journey. We made it to the store and bought the things we needed, including water for the boys for the trip home.

What a God we serve! He cares about us and what we are going through each moment. This incident taught me that there is no problem that is either too big or too small. They are all the same to Him, and He is only a prayer away.

We made it home without any further incident, recognizing just how real our God is. The experience also taught us to think before we act. Even though we had not been planning ahead or thinking about our future needs at that time, I thank God that He had a plan already in place. I am so happy that, even when we make mistakes, He does not abandon us. He loves you and me, and He is always willing to come to our rescue if we simply pray and trust Him.

The Big Blue Bus and the Sign

Wait on the LORD; be of good courage, and He shall strengthen your heart; wait, I say, on the LORD!
—**Psalm 27:14**

6 There was yet another big change in store for us! Little did we know this one would last for six long years and become the hardest of all for us as a family. Would we stand the test of our faith, which we would need to get us through? Our prayer was: God help us!

Our boys were happy and healthy and growing up quickly. They were now six and four. Our first-born was approaching school age, and we were trying to decide how we would handle his education. We believed in Christian education, so we started to look for the best Christian school for him to attend. The one we found he could only attend for a while, for it was too expensive for us to handle both the house and the school.

What were we to do? Where would we go? We did not know. We were on our knees often. We did not want to leave our nice house in which the kids were being raised, but our conviction was that Christian education had to come first. With God's help, we made our decision: we would sell the house. We were sad, but we knew in our hearts that it was the right thing to do.

Mark had the idea of buying a school bus and renovating it so that we could have enough money to pay for our boys' Christian schooling. He made it sound like fun! We would take the seats out, build beds, a shower, and closets. We would also put in a refrigerator and stove. For cold days and nights, we would have a gas heater. It would be just like a big motorhome when we were finished. We found the perfect seventy-two-passenger bus and began the renovations. Everything was going as planned. However, the boys did not like the change at all, especially our oldest. He did not want to leave our nice, comfortable house to live in a bus.

When the renovations were complete, it was time for us all to move in, including our cat. However, our timing was not perfect. We were living in Connecticut, and it was March. The snow was gently falling, and it was very cold. We started up the bus and slowly made our way to a campground that we knew was open all year. We had no heat in the bus, but we did have the gas heater, though the gauge on the heater registered empty. However, we knew we could fill it up when we arrived at our destination. The trip took us longer than we expected, so when we got there, everything was closed, including the place that sold gas for our heater. Needless to say, we were very cold that night. That was no fun for any of us. However, the next day, we were able to get the much-needed gas, and things started looking a lot brighter.

We stayed at that campground for about three months. That is not very long, but it was long enough for our boys to get into all kinds of trouble, as little boys will often do when given the chance. Around June, we found a nicer campground. Summer had arrived, and it was the perfect time for our family to be outside. We felt very blessed and believed that God was answering our prayers.

Then I found myself "in the family way" again with our third child. Oh no! What do we do next? We barely had space for the four of us. How were we going to make room for one more! Mark, resourceful as he is, built a crib-like cage in the back of the bus above our bed. It had bars across, and the door hung on hinges, so we could swing it down to open. It took a while to make the needed changes to the bus so that we could bring our new baby home.

It was August by this time, and our baby was not due until November. Meanwhile, we decided to go looking for an affordable house to rent for the winter months. We needed a more comfortable place to bring our new baby home to. We found a really affordable summer rental home on the ocean. It would be warmer than our bus. So, gathering everything we needed, including our cat, we moved into our new home. We also found a nice Christian school for our oldest to attend. When our third baby boy was born, it seemed to us that life could not be better. The month of June came around, and we headed back to the bus to start our new lives over again though, this time, with a bigger family.

Everything was going great except that our oldest son was not doing well at the Christian school he attended all winter. We needed to find another school for him to attend, one that would meet his needs better.

We were on our knees again praying for God's guidance, and God led us way up north to New Hampshire. That was quite a challenge! We were moving from warmer Connecticut to cold New Hampshire where we had some Christian friends who would allow us to park our bus on their land. As we did, we found a nice little Christian school connected with a great church for us to attend.

Life in the bus was very challenging at times, especially in the brutal winter of New Hampshire. We went through so many ups and downs, and there seemed to be more downs than ups, which included going through a major accident that almost cost us our lives. Yet, we knew that God had a plan, and, if we were going to survive, we had to stay faithful. God showed us time and again that He was with us, helping us through it all. Every time we faced a challenge, we prayed and God answered.

I remember one particular New Year's Eve when we were feeling down and hopeless about not ever getting out of the bus and were thinking that maybe it was where God wanted us to be. That was a very depressing thought, but we were trying very hard to accept whatever God's plan was for our little family, and we were trying to stay focused and happy no matter what. One winter evening, our water pipes were all frozen up, and we were getting ready for family worship. We knew that, after our worship, we would be heading out to our friends' house to take our baths before bedtime. Our youngest was in his bed with a fever. That night we thanked God for a roof over our heads and then asked God to show us a sign that somehow we would be leaving this situation soon. The kids were getting older; they were now eleven, nine, and four. Things were harder to handle in the bus. For sure, we all needed more space. So, while we were praying for God's sign, our frozen pipes started to thaw out, and, all of a sudden, water started coming through

> *That night we thanked God for a roof over our heads and then asked God to show us a sign that somehow we would be leaving this situation soon.*

the faucet, spitting like it does when the spring has begun. Wow! We could not believe what we were seeing. It was the dead of winter, on the top of a mountain in New Hampshire on New Year's Eve! We knew that there was no way that the outdoor pipes, which were surrounded by thick ice, could be melting by themselves. It was a miracle that we were witnessing! Amazingly, we took our baths that night in the bus. That was our sign. God was showing us, in a big way, that things were going to get better for us. The pipes did freeze again—after all, it was January—however, now we had hope that life was going to get better.

Shortly after that, God opened doors for us to finally leave the bus. We had lived through six long years of lessons that God wanted us to grow from. We witnessed major miracles that will stay with us for the rest of our lives. The experience taught us well how to adapt and live without material things. I looked at it as getting us ready for the time of trouble (Daniel 12:1), and I still thank God every day for that huge step we took. Thank you, God, for the power of prayer.

God shows us every day that He is alive! We just need to wait on Him and be patient. Put your trust in Him because He knows what is best for you.

The Prayed-for Home

*Delight yourself also in the LORD, and
He shall give you the desires of your heart.*
—**Psalm 37:4**

7

The long-awaited day of our big move finally arrived! We were going to leave the bus behind and move on! It seemed that God was opening the way for us to go to the state of Maine. Mark had a good job on the border of New Hampshire and Maine. Was God really calling us to make this move? All we could do was continue to pray and follow His leading.

Someone from the church in New Hampshire told us about a wonderful church school in Maine that had ten grades instead of the normal eight. We were thrilled! However, we really had to pray about it because we found out that Mark's work was quite a distance from the school. We decided to at least go and check it out to see if the school met the needs of our children.

I started researching who the teachers were and whether there would be anyone on site who could give us a tour of the school. I was thankful that I had a directory of all the right churches in that part of Maine. With a prayer on my lips that God would lead me, I started my search. I located an older couple that lived close to the school, and I proceeded to call them. They were so easy to talk with, and they knew all about the school since their own children had attended it years before. They had only great things to say about it. We met with them, and they introduced us to some of the school's teachers who gave us a great tour. We were sold! We truly believed that this was the best place for our children to be.

We went home all excited about the move. At that time, we were still living in the bus and going to church in New Hampshire. We loved our church family, and we knew it was going to be hard to say goodbye. One of our friends offered us a small camper for a reasonable price to help us make the move. We decided to buy it. The camper would at least give us a place to stay while we were looking for permanent housing. We hooked the camper to the back of the car and loaded all our belongings into it. The six of us—Mark and I, the three kids, and our cat—were ready for our new adventure.

And we were on our way! Yet, before leaving, we called the older couple we met in Maine, and they graciously offered to let us stay on their land while we looked for housing. We headed there, thanking God for all of His watchcare thus far. We arrived and stayed on their property a few nights before finding a nice campground, where we could park our camper close to the school. The kids were used to campgrounds, so they just loved it. Once again we began a search for the perfect place to live. Our friends told us about a trailer park not far away and encouraged us to go and check it out. The owner was a member of the church where we would be attending. The church was connected to the school. Wow! Everything was falling into place. There was a possibility that we could purchase a new mobile home to put in his trailer park. We met with him and his wife and made the purchase. He ordered it for us, and it would be ours after a short wait. It was exciting to know that we had a brand new mobile home coming!

It was August when we ordered the mobile home, and the months kept going by with no sign of it arriving. We were getting a little concerned, but we had to have faith that we would be in our mobile home before the dead of winter. A small camper is no place to be in Maine during the winter months. It was getting colder and colder in the camper, but finally, in November, our new home arrived. Whew! Talk about a close call. God knew our needs and saved us just in time from Maine's really cold weather. The new home was beautiful! We thought we were in heaven, especially coming out of the school bus and small camper. We learned to have patience and that all things can be difficult before they become easy. We were now ready for the next chapter in our lives, and we knew in our hearts that God does answer prayers. If you put your trust in Him and wait on His timing, then everything will come out better than you could ever expect.

A Promise of Hope

*It shall come to pass that before they call, I will answer;
and while they are still speaking, I will hear.*
—Isaiah 65:24

8

Our growing boys were getting older and turning hopefully into the men that Mark and I had envisioned them to be. However, their teenage years were not always easy. We wondered, Would they make it through? Each one of them would have to lean on God for all the decisions they were about to make. This is where I had to "let go and let God," and it was very difficult for me.

As our firstborn was growing up, it was getting harder and harder to raise him. He was very independent, and it seemed that any advice we gave him only caused more strife in the home. What should we do? I found myself many times on my knees praying for the wisdom of Solomon. Would we know how to handle every situation concerning him?

> *What should we do? I found myself many times on my knees praying for the wisdom of Solomon.*

We always attended camp meeting during the summer months with our children. These were very encouraging meetings that our kids loved to attend every year. In the early part of their lives, we would rent a tent to stay in at the camp meeting. We would prepare our clothes and food for at least ten days. It was a religious retreat, so not only were our recreational pleasures met but our spiritual needs as well. As the kids grew older, we stayed in the camper that we purchased when we moved out of New Hampshire. It always proved to be an enjoyable time. Our boys often helped get the camp meeting ready, which they loved doing.

I remember one particular camp meeting that proved, at the beginning, not to be so enjoyable. We arrived all happy, but then something dreadful happened! While we were there, my oldest son experienced a bad situation with his girlfriend, which made him very sad, and, from then on, his heart was just not into the camp meeting. He decided that he was going back home. One of his friends offered him a ride, and they left without telling any of us. It was not long before we found out what had happened. Mark immediately went to look for him and possibly bring him back.

I was so devastated that this could be going on with my son and that he was gone! I knew being with his friends at this time was not the answer. I retreated into our camper to pray that God would intervene some way. I prayed and cried to God, and I took my Bible for some comforting words. I opened my Bible and, without turning a single page, my eyes were drawn to Jeremiah 31:16 and 17. I read: "Refrain your voice from weeping, and your eyes from tears; for your work shall be rewarded, says the Lord, and they shall come back from the land of the enemy. There is hope in your future, says the LORD, that your children shall come back to their own border." What hope that was for me! God saw what was going on, and He assured me through His Word that everything was going to be okay. They did return that same night, and after praying with him, everything seemed to be all right for the time being. We had a great camp meeting, and we went home praising our God!

Things went well for a while; then, again, our son was making decisions that we did not agree with. He decided he was going to move out and live with some friends. Oh, my! That was not a good decision at all. I still did not approve of the friends he kept company with. However, he was approaching an age that he could do what he wanted, and we would have no say in the matter.

Then it happened—he left, and again I was so devastated that I went on the back deck with my Bible in hand to pray and plead for my son. I reminded God of what He had said a while back, how He was going to bring my son home and that I should not worry or cry. Here I was again, crying to God and telling Him that he is my son, and I can't just ignore it. I opened the Bible, and God brought me to the scripture that I needed to hear most—Jeremiah 31:20. "Is [this not] My dear son? Is he a pleasant child? For though I spoke against him, I earnestly remember him still; therefore My heart yearns for him; I will surely have mercy on him, says the Lord." What an answer! God was telling me that my son was *His* son too and that He also cries for him. I closed my Bible with a new understanding that God was in control and that I was to let it go. I was not sure how long it would take, but I was to trust Him completely to take care of the matter. Praise God! He was only gone for about four days. God does answer our prayers! Whatever you are going through, just give it to Him. He will hear your cries too and give you an answer before you even ask. Praise the Lord!

Our Beloved Cat Sam's Eulogy

Your mercy, O LORD, is in the heavens, and Your faithfulness reaches to the clouds. Your righteousness is like the great mountains; Your judgments are a great deep; O LORD, You preserve man and beast.
—Psalm 36:5, 6

9 Does God really care for all of His creatures that He created? Does He really care about the animals that make us so happy? Here is a sweet story that will answer these questions.

The first time we ever laid eyes on Sam was when we were living in New Hampshire in the school bus, raising our three boys. At the time, the kids were ten, eight, and three. We had been away all day, attending church and potluck and then visiting friends. We came home tired but happy, having spent a beautiful day. We all climbed in the bus and, to our amazement, there was a little yellow kitten sleeping on one of the beds. The boys were so excited!

We wondered how he had managed to get in, but, knowing that there were so many holes in the bus, it would not have been very hard for a little kitty to find his way in. Needless to say, that little kitty slept with my boys that night. He took a liking to our oldest and slept on top of him all night long. He would suck his white tee shirt as if sucking on a bottle. What a happy papa my son was! They all just loved Sam. The next morning, Sam found his way out of the bus and did not return again until evening to sleep and be loved. We never had to feed him for the longest time. He would go to a neighbor's home to be fed, and then he would come to us to be cuddled and loved all night.

Eventually, we started to feed him, and he became our cat. We called him Sam Spade, after the great detective, because he investigated his way into the bus and right into our hearts. However, he did not always have a good disposition. He could turn on us in a heartbeat, so we always had to be careful not to put our faces near him. Yet, we still loved our little Sam.

When we made our move out of the bus and into a house in Maine, we brought Sam with us. We had such happy times with him while the kids were growing up. He knew how to make us laugh with all of his funny antics. Like the rest of us, Sam was getting older. He was not as quick as he used to be. I noticed how he was putting on some weight, which was very unusual for him. He had always been a thin, healthy kitty. I knew something had to be wrong. I was so upset wondering what to do for him. Sam was starting to get worse, so I decided to take him to the vet to see if anything could be done. I knew if he had to be put to sleep then I would be the one facing the decision of having it done. I did not care for the way the vets put animals to sleep, and I had been claiming God's promise in Psalm 36:5, 6 that He loves the animals as much as He does people.

While we were at the clinic, the doctor opened him up and then explained to us how our kitty was so filled with cysts that there was nothing they could do for him. I told the doctor to put him to sleep while he was out on the table.

God is so merciful to His creatures. He heard my prayers. Now I did not have to make the decision to have the vet give him several shots, which would have been very traumatic for Sam. Instead he went to sleep peaceful and calm. We had him for a total of fourteen wonderful years. Unfortunately, the kids did not get to say "goodbye" because, at the time, they were grown up enough to have their own lives. It was such a sad time when they heard what happened, but we were all thanking Jesus for His watchcare over His creatures. He really does care!

We love you, my sweet Sam, and you will always have a special place in our hearts.

The Forks in the Road

*Trust in the LORD with all your heart,
and lean not on your own understanding;
in all your ways acknowledge Him,
and He shall direct your paths.*
—**Proverbs 3:5, 6**

10

Sometimes there are unexpected turns in the road we are traveling. Things in the LaPierre home were going on as usual. Raising three young boys brought daily challenges, which is expected. Not once could we imagine the big change that was soon to come for all of us. Actually, there were several changes on the horizon, and we would have to trust God to help us meet each one.

Our second child, Tim, was growing up and starting to think more and more on his own. This was the year of his eighth-grade graduation from the Christian school in the town where we lived. Things went well that year, and, as summer was approaching, we were anticipating going to another camp meeting. While we attended, Tim met a new friend, John, who lived close by. They hung out together, and John encouraged our son to go to the same Christian school as he did. It was a big decision, and it would require a lot of prayer. God seemed to be saying that this was a good change for him and that we should let him go. I did not like him going an hour away from us, but, with a heavy heart, we knew that this would be good for him. He would be starting ninth grade and living in a dormitory. That was the toughest year for me because, as a mom, I worried all the time that he was not getting the attention he needed, especially if he got sick. At times he would call, and I could tell how homesick he was in living away from us. We visited when we could, but it was not enough. After what seemed like an eternity, the school year was over. We had all made it through. Then he came home for the summer and found jobs to keep him busy.

During that summer the parents of my son's friend encouraged Tim to come and stay with them for the next school year instead of staying in the dorm. He liked that idea very much, and I did too. She was a great mom, and I could trust her and her husband with my son. God was truly answering our prayers. Everything was falling into place for him to continue going to that school, and his sophomore year proved to be even better for all of us.

However, another big change was about to happen in his junior year. Mark and I were offered a job at that school: we were to become dorm parents of seven boys, mine included! My son would move back into the dorm, and we would be a family again. That sounded wonderful to me. I would have all three of my boys back under the same roof. Mark and I were on our knees again, praying for God's guidance in all this. We had never taken care of seven teenage boys before, and we knew that, if this were going to work, we would have to spend a lot of time praying.

The day came for us to make the trip for our interview with the board. I was so nervous! We prayed that we would be making the right decision, and we were relying totally on God for the outcome of this interview. We arrived and found ourselves in a room with a handful of people who questioned all of our motives about why they should choose us to become the new dorm parents. We obviously answered all the questions correctly because, when we left, we had a new job. We were going to be the new dorm parents of this wonderful Christian school, and we could not believe it! We felt so honored and humbled at the same time!

We went home and started packing. We said our goodbyes for now to our wonderful friends, not knowing when we would be returning. We started out the school year with excitement and anticipation, totally unaware of what the future would hold, but knowing that God again was in control. That school year turned out to be very challenging, to say the least. We did a lot of praying for every situation that came up, and we knew that God would not let us down. Every day we thanked Him for the bigger family we now had to take care of. When the school year ended, we went back home just a little bit wiser than when we had started. I was praising God for those unexpected turns because they not only taught us more about trusting the Lord, but they turned out to be real blessings.

The Letter

Wait on the Lord; be of good courage,
and He shall strengthen your heart;
wait, I say, on the LORD!
—Psalm 27:14

11

Military life—just the sound of it made me unhappy. Our oldest son, Aaron, was approaching nineteen, and he still was not sure which direction he wanted to go. College life did not seem to fit him very well, but he still wanted to make something of himself. Then came the day that a military recruiter stopped by our home, trying to recruit young people. He made military life sound so appealing to my son that it did not take long for him to be hooked. Aaron did everything he could to get ready to join the Air Force, and Mark and I prayed that it would be the right decision.

At this time, he was showing no interest in God, and we were worried about his choices. We had to let go and let him find his own way, not ours. We had to trust that whatever path our son took God would be always with him. The military would either make him or break him. The day came when we had to say goodbye, and, with a prayer on our lips, we asked God to please protect our son. Then he was off for six weeks of basic training! We promised to write each other and to keep in touch. What would these six weeks hold for him? Would he be safe? Would he pass and graduate? I had so many questions and no answers. I had always heard bad stories about basic training. Were they true? Time would tell. I faithfully wrote letters to him, and I had to exercise patience in waiting for our first letter to arrive. Finally, it did arrive and, with anticipation, I began reading:

Dear Mom and Dad,

How is it going? Today is Sabbath, and I am starting my fourth week of training. Praise God! I am getting there! I never could have made it this far without God's help and your love! All your letters really help to keep me going. Please keep writing. Since I've been here I have seen one miracle in my life after another. No one could ever convince me that there is no God.

The first time I ever realized I needed Him was during PC. I had to run two miles without stopping. If I stopped I would be in serious trouble. After the first half a mile I thought I was going to die. Then by the end of the first mile, I knew for a fact I was going to die. It was then, for the first time ever, in a very long time, I prayed. I said, "If there is a God, please hear my prayers. I can't make it without your help. Please help me make it." A miracle then happened! Suddenly I felt a little more strength and a little less pain! I just kept praying for the whole second mile. With God's help, I made it! It took me 24 minutes and 40 seconds. The requirement to graduate in the sixth week is two miles in 18 minutes. Two days ago I did my third week running. We have been having PC three times a week and we have to run two and a half miles every time. On my third week running I ran the two miles in 16 minutes and 40 seconds. I went from 24/40 to 16/40 thanks to God's help. I still have to pray before I run or I cramp up every time.

I have a new Bible that I received when we left MEPS. They made us take it, and I thought I would never look at the thing. Well, I have been reading it every night before I go to bed. Every day I am more and more amazed by how God answers my prayers.

It is now Tuesday, and I am sitting at the shooting range waiting to practice shooting the M-16. It is a totally awesome machine gun! This morning I received a U for the week because I messed up dorm guard. If you receive two U's you will get recycled, which means I would have to go back to my second week of basic training. We can automatically get recycled for messing up dorm guard when we are in our fourth week, but once again, God helped me, and I only received one U.

This will be the worst week of training for us because one of our IT's, who was a student, just graduated and became an official IT. He will be getting most of this week off, so our team Chief SSGT is filling in for him.

He is the absolute worst one for recycling people. If you mess up at all, he will toss you! He has already threatened to recycle a bunch of people, and he did recycle two people. He has only been here two days.

Just keep praying that I will make it. He will be going back at the end of this week, so if I can just make it through this week, I think things will be okay. I keep praying every night and all day that I will make it. Pray for me too. Also pray that I will pass my red line inspections next week. If I fail those I will definitely be recycled. Well I have to go. I just received word that we will not be able to shoot because of an accident. We were also supposed to go camping tonight, but not sure if that will happen either.

I love you all. Keep praying and writing. I need all the help I can get from you and God. I will try to call again if I get another chance. Love you all very much and will see you soon.

Your Son.

Oh, how that letter warmed my heart as I heard that he was trusting God! I knew now that I did not have to worry so much about him. God had it covered. I was so thankful for the power of answered prayers. He does care about our wants and needs. We just need to wait on Him for all of our answers. We praised God for His watchcare over our son, and the best part was that he was finally learning to lean on Jesus. Praise God!

Tragedy Strikes the Family

But the salvation of the righteous is from the LORD;
He is their strength in the time of trouble.
—**Psalm 37:39**

12

Picture your loved one no longer able to take care of himself or herself due to a devastating illness. He or she is going to have to rely on someone else. Could that someone be you or me, even if we think, *I could never do something like that? I don't have the patience for it; it would overwhelm me.*

We don't have to be a professional caregiver to have the capability to fulfill the type of care giving that is placed before us. There are many of us who face this frightening issue every day. *Will it be my turn? Will I be placed in that position with one of my loved ones?* Little did I realize that very soon I would need God's strength more than ever to carry me through.

It was Christmas time! Mark and I and our youngest son decided to head out to Rhode Island to spend the holidays with my mom, sister, brother, and their families. We were excited about seeing everyone! Because we lived in Maine, a five-hour drive away, we only saw each other every once in a while. We arrived at my mom's home and had a wonderful Christmas Eve together. The following day we all went to visit her other children. It was such a great visit with everyone.

The next morning we got up, and my mom seemed to be in good spirits. I decided to help her with some chores before we headed home. We were making the bed together when suddenly she let out a scream and fell over onto the bed. She could not walk or talk any more. Mark and I helped her to a chair where we could assess the situation. It appeared that she had had a stroke. I called my sister who is a nurse and explained what was going on. She confirmed our suspicions and told us to get her to the hospital right away. We called an ambulance, and they came and took her. We followed by car along with her other children. So many questions were going through our minds. Is Mom going to die? Is she going

> *Is Mom going to die? Is she going to need long-term care now? If so, which one of us could take care of her?*

to need long-term care now? If so, which one of us could take care of her? We knew that she did not want to end up in a nursing home. All of my sisters and brothers worked except for me. If she did need the care, it looked as if it would be up to me.

God's mercy was manifested because, if we were not there at the time this happened, she would have been alone with no one to help her. I can't imagine what would have happened if we were not there at the right time. God knew, and He was watching over everything. For that, I am very thankful.

My mother spent five weeks in the hospital recovering. Her stay enabled us to go back home to figure out what we were going to do next. Her mind was still sharp, and, during those five weeks of recuperation, she was getting better. The only thing that was not getting better very quickly was her walking. Thankfully, her speech came back, and she was the same mom we knew and loved.

It was decided that I would go to Rhode Island to take care of her until she could walk again. After the five weeks of rehab, we went to pick her up from the hospital and to start our new lives together at her home. With a heavy heart, I said my goodbyes to Mark, knowing he could only come to visit on the weekends.

Every day was a challenge with Mom. I would take her through all the exercises that I was instructed to do with her, and very slowly she was gaining back her strength. She could finally walk with the help of a walker, and then with a cane. I read to her every morning from the Bible to try to keep her courage up. I knew God was with us, but it was unbelievably hard to be so long without Mark. I was with Mom for three long months. I prayed constantly for the strength and patience I needed to do my part no matter how long it took.

Mark called me every day, and, in one of those calls, he said that he had an interview for a new job in Virginia. Oh, my! That would mean another big change for us if he got the job, and I was thinking that it would be a change for the better. Mark went for the interview, and he got the job! When he called to tell me the news, we had such a mixture of feelings.

We not only felt excited, but we also felt apprehensive because we still had to deal with Mom. How could I leave her and go back to Maine to get ready for the big move? She was still not ready to live alone. There was so much for us to pray about. We believed that God gave Mark this new job, so now we would just have to trust God to work it all out.

    I called my brother to see if he and his wife could care for my mother for a short while, at least until we got settled in Virginia. He said, "Yes," and they traveled the sixteen hours from North Carolina to get her. Everything was falling into place for us to make the move. Everyone was happy except Mom because she felt in her heart that, once she left her home, it was possible that she would never be coming back. We could see her feelings in her eyes as she took one last look around her, saying her goodbyes. It was very sad for her. After our move, she would have a brand new life with Mark and me. We would be taking care of her from then on, and I would need all the strength that God could give me for whatever lay ahead. I praised God for all the answered prayers we had received thus far, and I did not doubt for one moment that He would be with me, supplying all the strength that I would need. I was learning that, if He calls you to do something, He will see you through it. Praise God!

Another Powerful Lesson to be Learned

For we walk by faith, not by sight.
—2 Corinthians 5:7

13

It had been a year since Mom came to live with us after her stroke. It had not always been easy with her, but God kept his promise to give me strength whenever I needed it. We were in Virginia now and living in a beautiful rental home that God gave us. We had felt like royalty in that home for the past year. The house was perfect in every way. Mom had her own space, almost like her own apartment, and we were feeling very content and blessed. Then suddenly, like an exploding bomb, the landlord informed us that the house was to be put up for sale. *Oh, no!* I thought. Where would we go? We did not have enough money to buy the house. In one quick second, we felt lost, and we knew that we were about to be homeless. People started coming to see the house, and it was not long before we had to leave. I asked God over and over, "Why?" Now that we had Mom, it was not so easy to move from one place to another. Again we found ourselves praying for the guidance that only God could give.

> *I asked God over and over, "Why?"*

We found a small apartment house with two bedrooms in it that was close to the old house. We were pleased with it because it would be easy to move all of our things there. However, it was not big enough to accommodate all of our belongings, so we had to rent a storage space. It was the saddest time for all of us, especially Mom. She really loved the house we had to give up, and now she was forced to live in a tiny little place, storing all of her treasured belongings out of sight. These were the only link she had to her life before the stroke. We all had major adjustments to make, but I think it was the hardest for Mom.

We knew we could not stay in the apartment indefinitely. It was too small, and it was costly to have to pay for rent and storage space. We needed a plan, and we needed it soon. We prayed to God continually for His help. We decided that we should start looking for a house to buy instead of renting. Day after day, we went house hunting with the realtor, searching for the perfect house to meet all of our needs. The search was exhausting—so many houses! Some of the ones we looked at met our criteria, but I knew in my heart that they were not for us. I always said, "When we find the right house, I will know it. God will tell me, 'This is the one.'"

After looking at so many houses and feeling that they were not the one, we were about to give up. There was a limit to the number for sale, and the prospect of finding the perfect house was growing dimmer and dimmer. One night we were at our apartment when a call came from our realtor telling us that she found a house that might meet all of our needs. When she told us where it was, my heart sank. The house was located in a bad part of town. I had heard stories about that area, and I was very hesitant to even look at the house. After praying about it, however, we decided to go and see it. We had nothing to lose and everything to gain. We found out that we would not be allowed to go inside the house since it was not yet up for sale. The realtor knew that it was going to be on the market soon and thought that we could be the first ones to make an offer. She encouraged us to at least go look at the area to see what we thought.

After much discussion, Mark, Mom, and I got into the car and headed for the house. If we were going to make a decision, we would have to check out the location. As we got closer to the neighborhood where the house was, my heart was getting excited! I felt right away that this was the one. The neighborhood looked really good and well kept. It was not far from a nice tourist town, so I knew the crime rate would not be bad here at all. We parked in front of the house and called the realtor to tell her to start making out the contract because we would be taking this house. We had no idea what the house looked like on the inside, but I knew that God was telling me that this was the one. Over and over again I felt it. Praise God! Our search was about to be over.

When we were finally able to see inside the house, I was immediately discouraged because it was in such bad condition. I questioned God's judgment, but I knew I had to take it regardless because He was telling me that this was going to be our home. I had to trust Him that He knew best.

It was not long before we could move in and start repairs. During the renovations, Mom looked so lost. We could not bring anything into the house until major repairs were done. There were walls that needed patching and painting, doors that needed replacing, and carpets that needed cleaning. In fact, every square inch of the house needed cleaning or repairing. It took us a while to get it all done, but, when it was finished, we were amazed! What a transformation! God knew that this would be the perfect home that we all needed at that time. I could not envision what it would become. What I saw at first was just awful. I needed faith to believe that God knew what He was doing, and I had to keep on walking by faith, trusting that things would turn out wonderfully in the end. Praise the Lord! Again I was learning a lesson. God was teaching me to walk by faith and not by sight. Hopefully, my mom was learning this lesson too. We took care of her for seven years, six of which were in this beautiful home that God gave us. I tried hard to show her that we serve a God who cares about our needs. Sadly, she died suddenly from complications with her bowels. I miss her very much. She was a wonderful mom to Mark and me and a wonderful grandmother to our children. I praise God for showing me how to keep walking without being able to see, holding His hand, and trusting Him to lead us in the right paths.

"Peaches," the Angel Kitty

*And He said to me, "My grace is sufficient for you,
for My strength is made perfect in weakness."
Therefore most gladly I will rather boast in my infirmities,
that the power of Christ may rest upon me.*
—**2 Corinthians 12:9**

14

July 2012. It was a beautiful sunny day in Newport News, Virginia! I was going about my day as usual, starting with the routine I had followed for as long as I can remember. I awoke to the alarm clock going off at 5:30 AM. Then I got up to fix my husband's breakfast and have worship time together before he headed off to work. As he left, I found myself alone to do all the things a busy housewife gets to do—the routine of laundry, cleaning, and other things. Mid-morning, I decided to go for a walk, so I called my sister, and the two of us went out to walk connected by our phones. As we were walking and talking, I started to feel a little dizzy and told my sister, who is a nurse. My sister told me that it was allergy time and to make sure that I took my Claritin. As the day went on, I kept on having dizzy spells. The next morning, I awoke with the woozy feelings still bothering me, though it seemed to be a little worse. I wondered what could be happening and prayed fervently about it. It did not cross my mind that I was about to embark on a big health change that would last many years.

A week had passed from that first dizzy spell, and it was now approaching the weekend. My head was feeling progressively worse. I knew that it would be a waste of time to call the doctor's office on the weekend when that is the hardest to get in to see him. I had several options to pursue. I could either go to the hospital or to a walk-in facility. I chose a walk-in facility that was not far from my house. I needed to do something quickly because I felt totally out of control. The dizziness kept me from walking without help, and there was so much pressure in my head that I felt that any moment it would explode. With my husband by my side, I went to a quick-care facility.

Once I had checked in, the staff called me in to assess my condition. They checked my ears and discovered that they were both full of fluid. That seemed to be the immediate problem, and I was so thankful that there might be a remedy for it. They prescribed all the proper medicine, and I went home to start taking it. I soon discovered that none of the medicines were helping but were, in fact, making my head feel worse.

I continued to pray to God to help me find a solution to my problem and, if it were possible, to relieve the awful pressure in my head.

I made appointments with my regular doctor and with an ears, nose, and throat doctor. By the time I went to see them, all the fluid seemed to have dried up, and the doctors could not explain why I was still feeling tightness like a belt around my head. It was almost like I was encased in a box. The wooziness was still so bad that I felt like I was always walking on a tilt. I also had bothersome noises in my ears. It was something I had never experienced before.

The weeks were going by, and I could not see that I was getting any better. I finally had an MRI done, and there was no explanation for what was going on. For the present, I would have to depend on a walker. Even my vision was impaired at times. I found myself walking around the house with that walker for many hours, never stopping, for, if I stopped, I felt like everything was still moving. I pleaded with God for the help that only He could give, but He seemed to be so very far away.

I heard about a very reliable health-conscious doctor who did not use drug therapy but only natural remedies. I gave him a call and began a rigid regimen of natural therapies. *Everything else had failed, so why not give this new way a try?* I thought. After months on the natural remedies, things started to feel a little better, but not much. Something else was going on, and all I could do was wait and pray.

One day, a very sweet church member and friend came over and gave me an "angel bell." She explained that whenever I felt out of control to just ring that beautiful bell, and my angel would be there right beside me. There were so many times I rang that bell and cried out to God for His help. People would come over to visit and pray for me but soon learn that their visits had to be short. Short visits were all I could deal with. To talk on the phone was also a chore. I had to leave it on speaker at the lowest setting or the awful pressure in my head would become worse. Life was so depressing that I could not see the light at the end of the tunnel.

After many months of suffering, I concluded that the fluid that was once in my ears had worked its way into my inner ear. The problem had to be that I had a defective inner ear. The fluid would build up and then very slowly dry out. My sister had had the same problem for five years, and my grandmother did too. As the fluid began to clear up, I had such an awful feeling of being disconnected that I had to drop to my knees and cry out to God: "When will this time of trouble and sickness ever end?" This was my constant question.

Through all of this, there was one bright spot for which I was very thankful. It was a little kitty by the name of "Peaches." I had seen the beautiful little kitty around for a few years now and had attempted to get close to her, but she never wanted to get close to anyone. The people that owned her had moved out of the neighborhood and, unfortunately, had left her to take care of herself. A few of the neighbors took it upon themselves to care for her, but she was definitely an outdoor kitty.

Sometimes I would go outside on the back deck with my walker to get some sun on my head and just sit and pray while feeling so woozy. One of those times, I saw Peaches out in the yard but just ignored her, as I always did. Peaches sensed something was wrong and started coming up on the deck to sit with me. This happened every day. Having Peaches near made me feel much better because now I was not alone. I had a kitty to talk to. It really helped me to get my mind focused on something else. We became great buddies for the next three years. By the time the kitty died, I did not need her so much anymore because I had begun to feel a little better. I am thankful to God for sending Peaches to me, just when I needed her most. I called her the "angel kitty," for she was truly God's little missionary to me. Through her, I could see that God was seeing and answering!

This bothersome sickness taught me to totally rely on God. It showed me the meaning of humility, for I could not resolve this situation myself. It was way too big. I thank God for allowing me to go through this experience because it has brought me one step closer to serving God the way that I should, knowing that I cannot rely on myself to get through each day. I have fought this illness for almost five long years, but I know now how much I need God, whether in sickness or in health.

Put all of your trust in God, and He will get you through your toughest situations. When you think positive thoughts, they will become healing thoughts. Praise God that He is only a prayer away!

The Finest Hours:
Preparing the Heart

Then I will give them a heart to know Me, that I am the LORD;
and they shall be My people, and I will be their God,
for they shall return to Me with their whole heart.
—Jeremiah 24:7

15

I could sense that something bad was happening to someone very close to me, but I wasn't sure how to handle it. Jim, my brother, was obsessing over everything, especially about his health. Sometimes he made needless big purchases that we were not accustomed to seeing him do. Then he started obsessing about his health to the point that he thought he was dying. His wife, Sally, and their two children were trying to figure out what was going on. So they took him from hospital to hospital, totally unaware of what awaited them in the end.

Every diagnostic came up negative. There was nothing wrong with him. The doctors told him that, for some reason, he was under tremendous stress and that he should go home and get some sleep. So, this once happy man, who lived life to the fullest with his family, was now losing a lot of weight, and, despite what the doctors' tests said, he believed he was dreadfully ill. All day and all night he would pace and wring his hands. He was slowly becoming a psychotic. What would his family do? He was on the verge of losing his reason.

Frequently Sally would be sitting in a hospital waiting room with the kids, texting me and the rest of the family what was happening while crying and feeling utterly helpless. Our only recourse was to give it all to God in prayer. We tried so hard to give Sally good advice, but nothing was working to ease her mind. Her once-happy home was falling apart around her, and there was not one thing anyone could do about it. This went on for about six months. Jim was out of work and had no income coming in. They were about to lose everything they ever owned.

The sad day came when things started to disappear, and he almost lost everything he owned. Most of us were unable to help them. Our wonderful uncle bought and paid for a vehicle so they could at least have a working car. However, it took several tries to get one that ran properly. Others helped with food. Some of Jim's siblings paid their bills, but this was all too much for anyone to take on alone.

All we could do was pray, and it seemed as if God was so far away. There seemed to be no answer to their desperate situation. Jim was getting worse, to the point that we thought that he was going to die. We were all preparing in our minds for a funeral. One day as I was crying and praying to the Lord, a thought came to me that perfectly described what was happening to this wonderful family. I imagined Jim and Sally and their kids on a beautiful ship. They were sailing on calm waters, and the sky was so blue and peaceful. Everything was great for a very long time. Then, all of a sudden, a big storm came up and blew out the engine side of the boat, when it is the engine that keeps the boat running smoothly. I thought of Jim as the engine. Water was coming in rapidly, and it wouldn't be long until the boat would start to sink and those on it would likely drown. They determined that there was not much they could do because the rescue boats onboard were too small to save them from the raging waters. They sounded the alarm and radioed all those they could of their impending doom. Few were in a position to come and save them, for they saw the dangers of the raging waters.

They prayed and prayed, and then brave souls, Jesus and His rescue team, the holy angels, responded to their call for help. He proclaimed, "I am going to go and answer that alarm."

Jesus starts toward them with His team. Can you see Him in the distance, walking on the raging waters? As He moves forward, He commands the waters to be calm, and they immediately obey. It takes a while to reach everyone in peril, but this is only because they all need time to believe that someone is going to rescue them. If it were to happen too fast, there would be no need for faith, when the team really needs to know that everyone confidently believes and does not get discouraged and die. Jesus needed to know that, when He arrives with the rescue team, they will be waiting for Him with open arms, thanking Him with all of their hearts and being truly grateful for their rescue.

We are going to call the experience I have been describing "the finest hours"—not the final hours. They are the finest hours because they are when hearts are being prepared to meet the rescue team when it arrives.

Knowing neither the day nor the hour, they need to hold on, exercising faith that rescue is coming because that is what Jesus has promised. He said He would never leave us or forsake us. Praise God, He was coming, and we were never to doubt that!

Jim ended up in a psychiatric ward in the hospital. In his depression, he had not showered or taken care of personal hygiene in months. The doctors finally gave him a choice—he could either be sent to a mental institution or he could receive electroconvulsive therapy (ECT), which were shock treatments used to treat certain types of mental illness. The doctors recommended ECT as the better option, believing that the shock treatments would bring him back to normal. Jim was not mentally stable enough to make the choice. He was afraid of the shock treatments, and, if he chose the mental hospital, he would not see his family as often as he had been used to. My whole family and many others were praying for this man. God was even then hearing and answering because he finally chose to sign the papers to begin treatment that same week. It was to be done on Friday, at 10:30 AM. We were praising the Lord because, if he had chosen the mental institution, he could have been there for up to a year or more. That was something that none of us wanted, and there would be little hope that he would improve.

Friday came. As I was having my early morning devotions and staying in prayer because of Jim's situation, I received a text from Sally saying that she was so depressed because Jim was backing out of his decision for fear that he was going to die. I told her to stay calm for God had the situation in hand, and I proceeded to pray and plead with God for answers. In those moments, I received such awesome answers and shared with Sally that God was answering me. She, in turn, felt the Holy Spirit working and her major depression lifting. Then she went to the hospital to share with Jim all that God had done that morning in hopes of encouraging him. When she arrived, she found him much more at peace than before. It was now about 8:30 AM. I decided to call my sister to let her know what was going on and to tell her how God was answering in such a big way. So many miracles were happening with all of the siblings at the same time, even with the ones who didn't believe and who never kept in touch. God connected with all of them in a minute or less and put us all together by phone in a split second. I truly believe God was showing us just how real He is, and he wanted Jim to know that the family was supporting him that very moment.

It was 10:15 AM, and the time was getting closer for him to have the procedure when I received another text from Sally saying that Jim was once again in a state of major panic. I texted her back and told her to stay calm, that God had this. Then, right at 10:30 AM, she texted me to say that he was in the middle of the procedure and that he went down peacefully.

Since that day, he has been improving so much. He is talking and laughing. He has had six ECTs in all and is now home and doing wonderfully. He is driving, eating, and gaining much-needed weight. He is working around the house and getting things done. His old self is coming back. The family is so thankful to Jesus and His rescue team for this major miracle, this transformation of a husband and father. They are truly grateful. They have worship time together, and they have all learned what it means to have the power of prayer on their side. Praise the Lord! God is awesome in His works for His children!

Dealing with Uncertainty

*Therefore I say to you, whatever things you
ask when you pray, believe that you receive them,
and you will have them.*
—Mark 11:24

16

It was the end of August, which meant that it was almost time for my yearly mammogram. I have gone for a mammogram every year since I was in my late 30s. I have always said that I wanted to keep myself healthy for my family's sake. My aunt died from breast cancer, so I really needed to be checked every year. In my early 50s, I had a scan that came back positive. I had a follow-up ultrasound that did not go well. The doctors could not find the questionable shadow and told me that I needed to go for a biopsy to really check it out. The word "biopsy" frightened me, and I really did not want to have it done. So I went home and prayed about it. Then I called them back and told them that I wanted two weeks for prayer and to make some changes in my diet, then I would go back for a third mammogram to see what God had done before I would have a biopsy.

They accepted my proposal, and I began pleading with the Lord for healing. I stayed away from many things I knew that I should not be eating. I did not want anything in my body that would contribute to the problem. I continued this way for the two weeks and then went for the scheduled mammogram, trusting completely in the Lord for the outcome of the test. When they completed the scans, they looked them over and came back to tell me that the questionable place had gone away and that I could go home. I thanked my God for all of His answers. Every year after that I have continued having a mammogram and have always received great results until my eighth year.

The year is 2017, and I am getting ready to go again for my yearly mammogram. Today there are better diagnostics to detect problems, like a 3D scan, but I always turn this scan down because it gives off a higher level of radiation and is a little more expensive. I had my regular scan and went home, not thinking anything about it. However, not long afterward, the dreaded call came, telling me that they wanted to see me again because the results of my scan were not good. I was concerned because I had noticed an unusual lump that had appeared a few months before.

I had thought about having it checked but had not gotten around to it. Now, with the mammogram results coming back positive, I was worried. They wanted me back in a few days, and I said, "No, I will schedule another mammogram for two weeks from now, so I can pray." The next two weeks found me on my knees, seriously talking with God and asking Him, if there were a problem, to please heal it. I told Him that I would do everything that I could to stay healthy if He would do His part and let everything be okay. I kept my part and prayed every day that God would keep His. I also mentioned to Him that I did not want an ultrasound because the last time I had had one, years before, it was really painful.

Two weeks later I went in for the scan. This time they performed a 3D scan. I told the female technician that I did not want an ultrasound because they had been very painful for me. She told me that all do-overs usually have an ultrasound, so I should be prepared. I kept telling her that I did not think that I would need one for I believed that God would honor my agreement with Him. I know that God sometimes says, "No," but I was staying strong and praying that God's will be done, knowing that God sometimes says, "Yes!"

After the test, the technician told me to sit in a little room with other patients who had to have their scans repeated. While I was sitting there, I prayed silently for each one of the ladies who would be undergoing the same procedure and who was experiencing the same uncertainty. The technician told me that I would have to wait a while, but it was not even five minutes before she returned with a broad smile. I said, "Well, I hope you are smiling for a reason." She told me to come with her, and, while we were walking, she said that I did not need an ultrasound because the questionable mass was gone, and I could go home. I felt like I was in a dream and had just stepped into the land of sunshine. Oh, the precious power of prayer! All that day I basked in God's love, witnessing to everyone I came in contact with how we serve an awesome God. I learned that day that there is nothing, including certain foods I might like, that is worth sacrificing my health for. I was praising Him for keeping His part, and I fully intend to always keep mine.

It is my prayer that, as you have read my stories, you have been able to see how real and caring God is and that, not only is He ready and willing to deal with your big problems, but He is also close at hand to help you with your little ones. He will answer you if you only trustingly come to Him in prayer.

TEACH Services, Inc.
P U B L I S H I N G
www.TEACHServices.com • (800) 367-1844

We invite you to view the complete
selection of titles we publish at:
www.TEACHServices.com

We encourage you to write us
with your thoughts about this,
or any other book we publish at:
info@TEACHServices.com

TEACH Services' titles may be purchased in
bulk quantities for educational, fund-raising,
business, or promotional use.
bulksales@TEACHServices.com

Finally, if you are interested in seeing
your own book in print, please contact us at:
publishing@TEACHServices.com
We are happy to review your manuscript at no charge.

www.ingramcontent.com/pod-product-compliance
Lightning Source LLC
Chambersburg PA
CBHW042134160426
43199CB00021B/2907